LOOM BANDS!

Fun accessories to make from colourful rubber bands

WHAT'S INSIDE

4 INTRODUCTIO

6 Rainbow Bracelet

10 Neon Wristband

14 BEADED BRACELET

18 Multicoloure Hairband

22 STRIPED KEY RING

26 Beaded Jewellery

30 Flower Bracelet

34 FUNKY FLOWER RING

38 Surfer Wristband

42 WILD WRISTBAND!

46 Tips & Tricks

47 Further Reading

48 ACKNOWLEDGEMENTS

JOIN THE LOOM BAND FUN

Loom bands are the latest trend to arrive from the US. Starting right now you can make your own fabulous accessories using these tiny, brightly coloured rubber bands by following the instructions given in this book. Apart from the loom bands, all you need is a hook and two pencils, or a fork or a Rainbow Loom® and you're good to go! You'll find lots of different techniques used across these projects to create the various looks that can be achieved with loom bands. So why not get started right away? However, be warned. Once you start, you'll never want to stop! We know that from experience. Just make sure that you always have plenty of spare rubber bands to hand. Have fun and enjoy making lots of cool fashion accessories.

Heike Roland   Stefanie Thomas

RAINBOW BRACELET

SIMPLE WRISTBAND MADE WITH PENCILS

WHAT YOU NEED: 4 rubber bands in each of the following colours: white, yellow, orange, pink, red, apple green, grass green, turquoise, medium blue, dark blue, dark lilac and pale lilac (48 rubber bands in total) • clip • 2 pencils

1 This technique can be used when out and about. Wind a white band around two pencils in a figure of eight, keeping the pencils close together.

2 Now push two more bands (we used a yellow one followed by an orange one) over the pencils without twisting them.

3 Take hold of the bottom loop (the white one here) on the right pencil with your finger (or you can use a hook) and pull it to the side ...

4 ... and then lift it over the end of the right pencil into the middle.

5 Then take hold of the bottom loop (the white one here) on the left pencil and pull it to the side ...

6 ... and then lift it over the end of the left pencil into the middle between the two pencils.

7 Push the two bands left on the pencils down a little and pull another bands (the pink one here) over the pencil ends. Make sure that you keep the bands in the colour sequence as given in the list of materials, and don't mix up the sequence of the three bands on the pencils.

8 Now pull the two loops of the bottom band (the yellow one here) over the pencils as described in steps 3–6. Then put another band (a red one) over the two pencils as described in step 7. Keep repeating steps 3–7, making sure that you first put a third band over the two pencils before you lift the two bottom loops over the pencil ends and position the band between them.

9 Repeat the colour sequence four times until all the bands are used up. Lift the bottom loops off the pencils ...

10 ... until only one loop is left on each pencil.

11 Put one side of the clip through the loop on the right pencil ...

12 ... and then through the band on the left pencil and slide out both of the pencils.

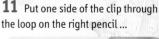

TRY THIS!
This fishtail bracelet also looks great if you make it in two colours! Keep alternating red and white rubber bands, for example; your bracelet will then be made up of very thin rings of colour. If you want the strips of colour to be thicker, use three (or more) rubber bands of the same colour in succession, and then change to a different colour.

13 Lastly put the two loops of the first band (the white one here) into the other side of the clip. You now have a fabulous rainbow-coloured fishtail bracelet!

TOP TIP!

You can make this bracelet as long as you like. If you use double the number of rubber bands, you can either wrap it around your wrist twice or wear it as a necklace around your neck. You can also make fishtail bracelets on the Rainbow Loom®. Instead of the pencils, simply use two neighbouring pegs on the Rainbow Loom® and follow the given instructions here.

NEON WRISTBAND

EASY ARMBAND MADE USING A FORK

WHAT YOU NEED: 35 rubber bands in neon green • 16 rubber bands in neon pink • clip • fork • hook

1 Take the fork in your hand. Place a band (green here) over the two left tines of the fork in a figure of eight. Place a second band (green here) in a figure of eight over the two right tines.

TOP TIP!

When making this bracelet, always make sure that the rubber bands that you place over the fork are pulled tightly to the back of it. You must also hold the rubber bands firmly on the back of the fork with your index finger to prevent them from sliding off.

2 Now place another band (pink here) around the two middle tines of the fork, again in a figure of eight.

3 Pull the bands tightly to the back and hold them in place with your index finger. Now pull first one and then the other bottom loop of the bands (the green ones here) that are in front of the middle tines of the fork, over the middle tines to the back of the fork.

4 Now pull all the bands tightly to the back. From now, the bands are placed over the tines of the fork straight, rather than wound in figures of eight.

5 Place another band (the green one here) over the two right and the two left tines of the fork.

6 Hold the bands tightly to the back of the fork and lift all of the loops in front of the fork (green-pink-pink-green here) ...

7 ... over the tines in turn and to the back of the fork.

8 Don't forget to pull the bands tightly to the back of the fork every time you move one. Now there will only be four rubber bands over the front of the tines.

9 Place the next rubber band (the pink one here) over the two middle tines and lift the bottom loops (the green ones here) over the middle tines to the back of the fork (see step 3). Repeat steps 5–9 until you have used up all the bands or the wristband is the length you want it to be.

10 Now lift the two outer loops onto the middle tines of the fork.

11 Continue working on the back of the fork: transfer the four remaining loops from the tines on to a hook. Take another band (the green one here) onto the the end of the hook ...

12 ... pull it through all four loops ...

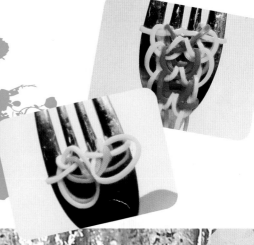

TOP TIP!

Don't worry if the rubber bands on the back of the fork look a little "chaotic" to start with! After a few rounds you'll start to see how fabulous your wristband is going to be.

13 ... and then place the other end of the band on to the hook.

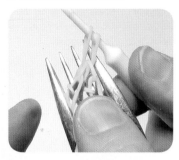

14 Now take the wristband off the fork and put the clip through the two loops on the hook.

15 Stretch the first three bands of the wristband over your index finger and hook the other end of the clip into these loops. Now you have a seriously cool fork wristband.

TRY THIS!

You can use this technique to weave a cool belt that looks great worn over a T-shirt or with jeans. Try different colour combinations to suit your outfits.

BEADED BRACELET

DELUXE BRACELET WITH ADDED BEADS

WHAT YOU NEED: 28 rubber bands in lilac • 10 rubber bands in black • about 8 rubber bands in lavender (depending on the circumference of your arm, to extend the bracelet • letter beads with large holes (maximum 10) • clip • Rainbow Loom® • hook

NOTE: On the left inside cover flap of this book is a handy photo of the loom with numbered pegs.

1 Stretch a lilac band over pegs 1M and 1L on the Rainbow Loom®.

2 Continuing down the left-hand row of pegs, stretch lilac bands between each of the pegs until the last peg but one. So, first stretch a band from peg 1L across to 2L, then from 2L to 3L and so on. Place the last lilac band on the left-hand side from 12L across to the middle row and 13M.

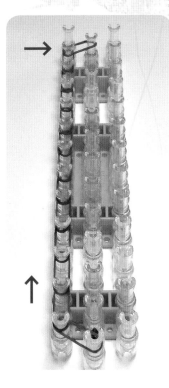

3 Repeat steps 1–2 along the right-hand row. Start at peg 1M and stretch a band across to peg 1R, then from 1R to 2R, then from 2R to 3R and so on. Stretch the last band from 12R across to 13M. Pegs 13L and 13R are not used.

4 Wrap a lilac band twice around peg 13M. Push all the bands down on the pegs. This will give you more room on the pegs for the next bands.

5 Push a black band through each letter bead, leaving a loop hanging out on each side. There's room on this bracelet for a total of ten beads. If your name doesn't have that many letters either use the remaining black bands without beads (as shown here) or put coloured beads on them. We have chosen a name with seven letters. Start by placing a black band around pegs 2L and 2R in a figure of eight. Place the next black band around pegs 3L and 3R in the same way.

6 Then place the black bands holding the beads on the pegs. These do not have to be twisted in to a figure of eight. Start with the last letter of your name, and place the band from peg 4L to 4R. Continue like this until all the letters of your name are on the Rainbow Loom®. You will be left with one black rubber band. Place the last black band around pegs 11L and 11R in a figure of eight.

7 Turn the Rainbow Loom® around. Start weaving the rubber bands at peg 1M, as described for the basic bracelet (see the inside covers). Move the hook through the peg, under the two top lilac bands to the outside, then take up the top of the two lilac bands below and pull it to 2L.

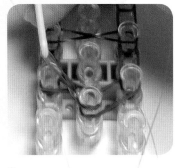

8 Then push the hook through the same peg again, under the two top bands to the outside, take up the lilac band below them, and pull it to 2R.

9 Weave together all the lilac bands on the left-hand row of pegs in turn. Start with peg 2L to 3L, then 3L to 4L and so on. Always insert the hook from above, not the side, into the peg to which you moved the last band, and take up the lower lilac band.

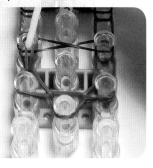

Repeat this step until you reach the end of the Rainbow Loom®. The last two weaves are 12L to 13L and 13L to 13M.

10 Now it's time for the lilac bands on the right-hand row. First weave 2R to 3R, then 3R to 4R and so on. At the end of the loop, weave 12R to 13R and 13R to 13M.

11 Your Rainbow Loom® should now look like this.

12 Using the hook, draw a lilac band through all the loops on peg 13M …

13 … and slide the two loops on to the hook.

14 Then slide the bracelet off the Rainbow Loom® and weave about eight lilac bands together, either with the Rainbow Loom® or the hook – as explained on the inside right cover – to make an extension so that the bracelet fits comfortably around your wrist. Secure the bracelet with a clip.

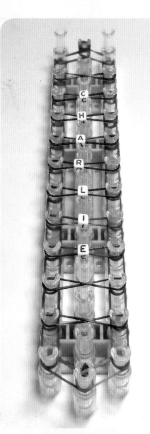

10

11

12

13

TOP TIP!

You can choose from glass, plastic, wood or letter beads. They may be faceted, opaque or translucent. What is important when choosing them is to make sure that the rubber band fits through the centre hole – everything else is completely up to you!

MULTICOLOURED HAIRBAND

ADJUSTABLE ALICE BAND

WHAT YOU NEED: 12 rubber bands in pink, blue, yellow and orange • about 26 rubber bands in pink (to extend the hairband to your head size) • clip • Rainbow Loom® • hook

NOTE: On the left inside cover flap of this book is a handy photo of the loom with numbered pegs.

1 Stretch a blue band from peg 1M across to 1L, and then a pink band from peg 1M to 1R.

2 Now stretch an orange band from peg 1L to 2M, and a yellow one from 1R to 2M.

3 Repeat steps 1 and 2 for the remaining pegs until you get to peg 13M. Make sure you get the sequence of the bands right! So the next bands are placed as follows: 2M to 2L, 2M to 2R, 2L to 3M and 2R to 3M, and so on. Pegs 13L and 13R are not used. Wrap a pink band twice around peg 13M.

4 Turn the Rainbow Loom® around. Using the hook, pick up the yellow band from peg 1M and pull across to 2L (see Basic Bracelet on the Rainbow Loom®, left inside cover, step 7).

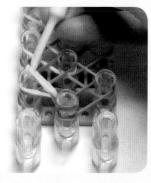

5 Now pick up the orange band from peg 1M and pull it across to 2R.

6 Take the pink band from 2L to 2M ...

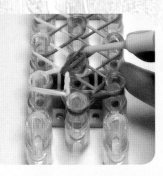

7 ... and the blue band from 2R to 2M.

8 Repeat steps 4–7 on the following pegs. Start with 2M to 3L (yellow), then 2M to 3R (orange), 3L to 3M (pink) and 3R to 3M (blue). Continue until you get to the end of the loom. Make sure you get the sequence of the bands right! Your loom will now look like this (see photograph on the right).

9 Using the hook, draw a pink band through all the loops on peg 13M ...

10 ... and slide the two loops on to the hook.

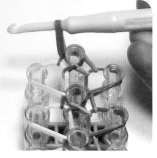

11 Then slide the hairband off the Rainbow Loom® and – as explained on the inside cover – weave about 13 bands together, either with the Rainbow Loom® or the hook, to make an extension so that the hairband fits comfortably around your head. Hook one side of the clip into the two loops of the last band.

12 Transfer the two pink bands at the other end of the hairband to your hook and link the second half of the extension on this side, also from 13 pink bands. Hook on the clip.

TRY THIS!

Make a matching bracelet or hair tie using this same technique. All you need to do is adjust the length of the band you make. This set is great either to wear yourself or to give to your best friends made in their favourite colours.

STRIPED KEY RING

STREET-STYLE KEY CHARM

WHAT YOU NEED: 13 rubber bands in black • 12 rubber bands in each of the following colours: lilac, pink and yellow • metal split ring key ring • Rainbow Loom® • hook

NOTE: On the left inside cover flap of this book is a handy photo of the loom with numbered pegs.

1 Stretch a lilac band from peg 1R to 2R, a yellow band from 1M to 2M and a pink band from 1L to 2L.

2 Continue along the rows with the same colours, working from front to back. So along the right-hand row place lilac bands from 2R to 3R, from 3R to 4R, and so on. Your Rainbow Loom® should now look like this.

3 Next stretch a black band in a triangle around pegs 2R, 2M and 2L. Place the next band around pegs 3R, 3M and 3L, then around 4R, 4M and 4L, and so on until you get to pegs 12R, 12M and 12L.

4 Wrap the black band twice around pegs 13R, 13M and 13L. This will give you a neater finish to the key ring.

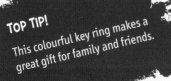

TOP TIP!
This colourful key ring makes a great gift for family and friends.

5 Turn the Rainbow Loom® around. Using the hook, pick up the pink band on peg 1R and pull it across to 2R (see Basic Bracelet on the Rainbow Loom®, left inside cover, step 7).

6 Pick up the yellow band on peg 1M and pull it across to 2M.

7 Now pick up the lilac band on peg 1L and pull it across to 2L.

8 So that you don't forget any of the bands it is best to work along an entire row before moving on to the next row. In other words, start with the left-hand lilac row and pull the bands from 2L to 3L, then 3L to 4L, and so on, until you reach the end of the row. Repeat these steps with the yellow bands in the middle row, then finally the pink ones on the right-hand row. The black bands are not used.

TRY THIS!

How about a wristband in the same pattern? Simply use the Rainbow Loom® or hook to make a bracelet extension as explained on the inside cover, step 11. You will also need to add a clip.

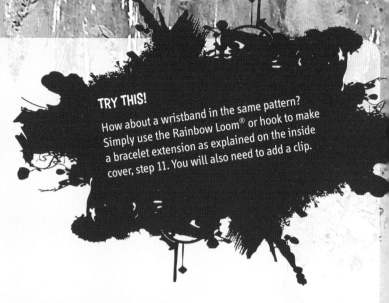

9 Lift the two pink loops from peg 13R across to 13M ...

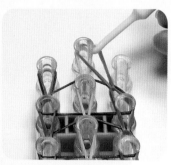

10 ... and the lilac loops from peg 13L to 13M.

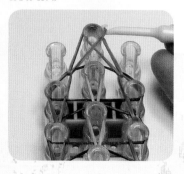

11 Using the hook, draw a black band through all six different coloured loops on peg 13M.

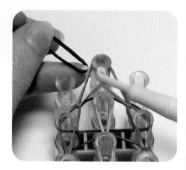

12 Place the two black loops onto the split ring and slide the finished keyring charm off the Rainbow Loom.®

TOP TIP!

If you would like to make a bracelet with horizontal stripes place three bands in the same colour beside each other on pegs 1L and 2L, 1M and 2M and 1R and 2R. Repeat this step with three bands in a different colour on the next pegs until you reach the end of the loom. Work steps 3–12 as explained on pages 22–24.

BEADED JEWELLERY

MATCHING PENDANT AND EARRINGS

WHAT YOU NEED: 14 rubber bands in each of the following colours: black and gold • black glass beads, 15mm in diameter • satin or leather cord, 50–115cm long, for pendent • earring hooks, for earrings • Rainbow Loom® • hook

NOTE: On the left-hand inside cover is a handy photo of the loom with numbered pegs.

1 Take a black band and a gold band and stretch the pair of bands together from peg 1M across to 2M.

2 Stretch the next pair of black and gold bands from peg 2M to 2L, …

3 … then 2L to 3L, 3L to 4L, 4L to 5L, 5L to 6L and from peg 6L to 7M.

4 Next stretch a pair of bands from peg 2M across to 2R. Now place the pairs of black and gold bands along the right-hand side of the Rainbow Loom® as you did on the left-hand side, from peg 2R to 3R, 3R to 4R, 4R to 5R and from 5R to 6R. Place a pair of bands from peg 6R to 7M.

TOP TIP!

When making this pendant design, always use two different colour bands held together as a pair when placing them over the pegs.

5 At the end of the round, wrap a gold band twice around peg 7M. Next thread a black band through the black glass bead and stretch the loops on either side of the bead over pegs 4L and 4R. Turn the Rainbow Loom® around.

6 With this design, only some of the pegs are covered with bands whilst other pegs are not used. When weaving, start counting from the first peg covered with a band, rather than from the beginning of the loom. So the first peg in the left-hand row with a band is 1L. Using the hook, pick up the top pair of bands beneath the gold loops on peg 1M and pull them across to 1L.

7 Now pick up the bottom pair of bands on peg 1L and lift them across to 2L. Weave the remaining pairs of bands along the left-hand row in the same way, from 2L to 3L, 3L to 4L, 4L to 5L and finally 5L to 6M.

8 Now it's time to weave the row on the right. Using the hook, pick up the pair of bands beneath the gold loops on peg 1M and pull them across to 1R. Weave the remaining pairs of bands in turn, finishing with peg 5R to 6M.

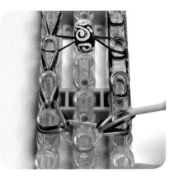

9 Your loom should now look like this.

10 Pick up the bottom pair of bands on peg 6M and pull them across to 7M.

11 Insert the hook through all the loops on peg 7M. Slide the loops onto the slightly thicker part of the hook and carefully remove the pendant from the loom.

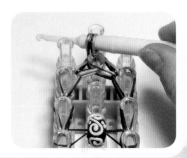

12 Move the loops back onto the front part of the hook, and pull the two left-hand loops through the two right-hand loops. Now pull these remaining loops tight so that the bands all tighten up and the pendant cannot come undone. Thread the leather or satin cord through these last loops to make a necklace.

TRY THIS!

Use the same technique (but without the bead) to make earrings to match your pendant. Starting with a single black band (instead of a pair of bands), work steps 2–4 as before but only using the left and right sides of the loom as far as pegs 5L and 5R. Place the last two pairs of bands from 5L to 6M and from 5R to 6M. Wrap the gold band twice around peg 6M. Now work steps 6–12 as before. To finish, put the loop of the earring in the eyelet of an earring hook.

FLOWER BRACELET

DECORATIVE FLORAL WRISTBAND

WHAT YOU NEED: 13 rubber bands in pink and lilac • 12 rubber bands in green and white (depending on the circumference of your arm, to extend the bracelet) • clip • Rainbow Loom® • hook

NOTE: On the left inside cover flap of this book is a handy photo of the loom with numbered pegs.

1 For the bracelet, work a total of six flowers in the colour sequence pink–green–lilac–pink–green–lilac. Start with six pink bands for the first flower. Stretch a pink band from peg 1M across to 1L and from 1M to 1R.

2 Now stretch a pink band from 1L to 2L and from 1R to 2R ...

3 ... then from 2L to 3M and from 2R to 3M.

4 Next, stretch a white band in a figure of eight over pegs 1L and 1R and a second one around pegs 2L

and 2R. The first flower is now ready.

5 Work the second flower in the same way, but start by stretching the green bands from peg 3M. So stretch the first green band from 3M across to 3L, then from 3M to 3R, 3L to 4L, 3R to 4R, 4L to 5M and 4R to 5M. Make sure you follow this exact sequence.

6 Work the remaining four flowers in the same way. Each time start the next flower on the peg in the middle row where the previous flower has just ended. Next, wrap a pink band twice around peg 13M. Pegs 13L and 13R are not used. Your loom should now look like this.

7 Turn the Rainbow Loom® around. Using the hook, pick up the top lilac band beneath the two pink ones on peg 1M and pull it across to 2L (see Basic Bracelet on the Rainbow Loom®, left inside cover, step7).

8 Now lift the other lilac band off of peg 1M and pull it across to 2R.

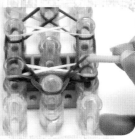

9 Weave together the lower of the remaining lilac rubber bands (not the white ones): 2L to 3L, ...

10 ... 2R to 3R, ...

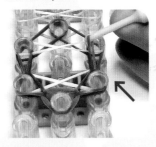

11 ... 3L to 3M ...

12 ... and finally 3R to 3M.

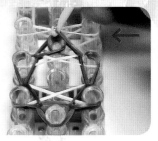

13 Repeat steps 7–12 for the remaining flowers. Start the second flower with 3M to 4L, and so on.

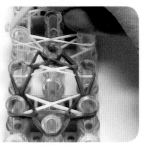

14 Your loom should now look like this.

15 Using the hook, draw a lilac band through all the loops on peg 13M. Lift the bracelet off the pegs and weave about eight bands together, either with the Rainbow Loom® or the hook, (see the right inside cover) to make an extension so the bracelet comfortably fits your wrist. Secure the bracelet with a clip.

TRY THIS!

By adding an extension to the Flower Bracelet, as described on page 20, steps 11 and 12, you can make a great matching hairband.

FUNKY FLOWER RING

FLOWER RING

WHAT YOU WILL NEED: 6 rubber bands in lilac and pink • 3 rubber bands in green • 1 rubber band in yellow • clip • Rainbow Loom® • hook

NOTE: On the left inside cover flap of this book is a handy photo of the loom with numbered pegs.

1 Stretch a green band from peg 1M across to 2M. Now start positioning the lilac bands from 2M to 2L, from 2M to 2R, ...

2 ... 2L to 3L, 2R to 3R, ...

3 ... 3L to 4M and 3R to 4M.

4 Working clockwise, stretch the six pink bands from peg 3M outwards in the shape of a star: stretch the first band from 3M across to 2L, the next ones between 3M and 3L, 3M and 4M, 3M and 3R, 3M and 2R ...

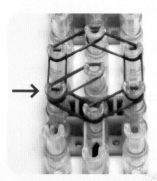

5 ... and the last one between 3M and 2M. Take care not to mix up the sequence of bands on peg 3M.

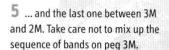

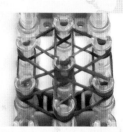

6 Place the first of the two remaining green bands over pegs 4M and 5M, and the second one over 5M and 6M. Wrap the yellow band twice around peg 3M.

35

7 Turn the Rainbow Loom® around and start weaving. With this design, only some of the pegs are covered with bands whilst other pegs are not used. When weaving, start counting from the first peg covered with a band, rather than from the beginning of the loom. So the first peg in the left-hand row with a band is 1L, the first one in the middle row is 1M, and the first one in the right row is 1R. Pull the green band from 2M across to 3M.

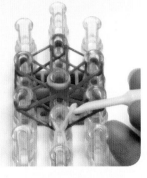

8 Insert the hook in to the middle of the flower (peg 4M) and pick up the first pink band beneath the doubled-up yellow band. Carefully pull it up (holding on to the yellow band so that it doesn't slide off the peg) and move it across to peg 5M. Continue in this way, working anti-clockwise, to pull

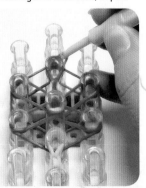

all the petals from the middle of the flower to the outside. Always pick up the pink band that is directly beneath the doubled-up yellow band, 4M to 2L, 4M to 1L and so on.

9 Your Rainbow Loom® should now look like this.

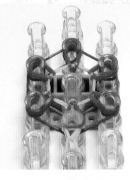

10 Now weave the lilac bands. First lift the top of the two lilac bands on peg 3M to 1L, and then the bottom one to 1R.

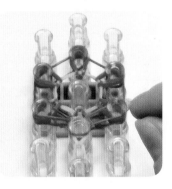

11 Then lift the bottom lilac bands following this sequence: 1L to 2L, 1R to 2R, 2L to 5M and 2R to 5M.

12 Then pull the green band from peg 5M to 6M.

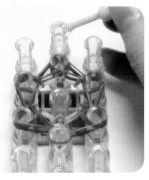

13 Hold the two green bands on peg 6M slightly away from the peg with your fingers and place over one side of the clip (see Basic Bracelet on the Rainbow Loom®, left inside flap, step 3).

Now slide the ring off the Rainbow Loom®. Hook the first green band on the other side of the ring in the clip.

TRY THIS!

Make this ring in lots of different colour combinations. You can always wear more than one colourful ring at the same time for maximum impact.

SURFER WRISTBAND

COOL COLOURFUL BRACELET

WHAT YOU NEED: 40 rubber bands in black • 22 rubber bands in turquoise • 12 rubber bands in apple green • about 8 rubber bands in black (depending on the circumferece of your arm, to extend the bracelet) • clip • Rainbow Loom® • hook

NOTE: On the left inside cover flap of this book is a handy photo of the loom with numbered pegs.

1 Stretch a black band from peg 1M across to 1L. Continuing down the left-hand row of pegs, stretch black bands between each of the pegs until the last

peg but one. So, first stretch a band from peg 1L across to 2L, then from 2L to 3L and so on as far as 11L to 12L. Now place a black band from 12L across to 13M. Peg 13L is not used.

2 Repeat step 1 along the right-hand row. Starting at peg 1M, stretch a black band across to peg 1R, then from 1R to 2R, then from 2R to 3R and so on as far as 11R to 12R. Place the last black band between 12R and 13M. Peg 13R is not used. Your Rainbow Loom® should now look like this.

3 Place a green band over pegs 1M and 2M.

TOP TIP!

With this technique, you will have lots of rubber bands on every peg on the loom, so it is very important to push them well down once they are in place. Take care not to mix up the sequence of the rubber bands on the pegs.

4 Now stretch a turquoise band from 2M across to 2L and another one from 2M to 2R.

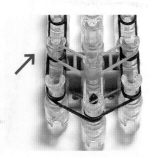

6 Now wind a black band twice around every peg on the middle row. Turn the Rainbow Loom® around.

8 Now link the top turquoise band by moving it from peg 2M across to 2L.

5 Repeat steps 3 and 4 on all the subsequent pegs until you reach the end of the loom. So place a green band between 2M and 3M, and then the next two turquoise bands from 3M to 3L and from 3M to 3R and so on. At the end of the loom, stretch the last green band from 12M across to 13M. Pegs 13L and 13R are not used. Make sure you follow the exact sequence so you can weave the bands together.

9 Then pull the bottom turquoise band from peg 2M across to 2R.

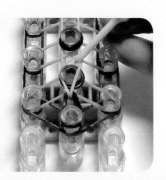

7 Using the hook, pick up the green band beneath the doubled-up black band on peg 1M. Carefully pull it up (holding on to the black band so it doesn't slide off the peg) and move it across to peg 2M (see Basic Bracelet on the Rainbow Loom®, left inside cover, step 7).

10 Repeat steps 7–9 until you get to the end of the loom. Make sure you follow the exact sequence so you can weave the bands together. So always lift the first green band up onto the next peg, and then weave the two turquoise bands forward. Pull the top of the two bands to the left, and the second one to the right. Finish with the last green rubber band, lifting it from 12M to 13M.

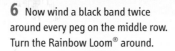

11 Now weave the black bands. Starting with peg 1M , lift the third band (counted from the top) to 2L.

12 Then pull the bottom black bands from 2L to 3L. Repeat this step with all the following pegs on the left-hand row until you get to 12L to 13L and 13L to 13M. Do the same on the right-hand row. Starting back at peg 1M, lift the bottom band to 2R. Lift 13R to 13M. Your Rainbow Loom® should now look like this.

13 Using the hook, draw the last black band through all the loops on peg 13M.

14 Lift the wristband off the pegs and weave about eight bands together, either with the Rainbow Loom® or the hook (see the right inside cover) to make an extension so the wristband comfortably fits your wrist. Secure the wristband with a clip.

WILD WRISTBAND

ZIP-EFFECT BRACELET

WHAT YOU NEED: 26 rubber bands in black • 24 rubber bands in white • 14 rubber bands in red • about 8 rubber bands in red (depending on the circumferece of your arm, to extend the bracelet) • clip • Rainbow Loom® • hook

NOTE: On the left inside cover flap of this book is a handy photo of the loom with numbered pegs.

2 Stretch a white band from 1L across to 2M and from 1R to 2M.

3 Stretch green bands from 1L to 2L and from 1R to 2R. Then place a red band over pegs 2M and 3M.

1 Stretch a green band from peg 1M across to 1L, then a red band from 1M to 2M, then another green band from 1M to 1R.

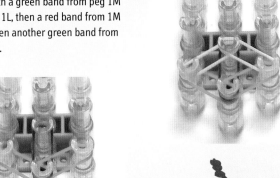

TOP TIP!

With this technique, you will have lots of rubber bands on every peg on the loom, so it is very important to push them well down once they are in place. Take care not to mix up the sequence of the rubber bands on the pegs.

4 Repeat steps 2 and 3 until all of the pegs have rubber bands in place. Place the next white bands over 2L and 3M, 2R and 3M. Then place the green bands over 2L and 3L, 2R and 3R, and a red band over 3M and 4M. After placing the last two green bands, stretch a red band over pegs 13L, 13M and 13R. This will create a triangle shape at the end of the loom.

6 Now lift the red band from peg 1M to 2M.

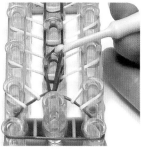

8 Now weave the green bands together. Using the hook, pick up the band on peg 1L and lift it over to 2L. Do the same with the bands all the way down the left-hand side. Always pick up the bottom band until you have lifted the last green band in this row from 13L to 13M. Weave the green bands on the right-hand row in the same way. Start with peg 1R to 2R and so on and continue to 13R to 13M.

7 Repeat steps 5 and 6 with the next pegs and bands, so 2M to 3L, 2M to 3R, 2M to 3M, and so on until you get to the end of the loom (12M to 13L, 12M to 13R and 12M to 13M). Your loom should now look like this.

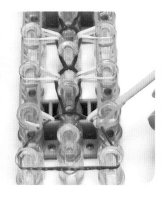

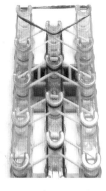

5 Turn the Rainbow Loom® around. Using the hook, pick up the top white band on peg 1M and pull it up and left to 2L. Then pull the other white band up and right to 2R.

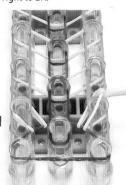

9 Your loom should now look like this.

10 Using the hook, draw the last red band through all the lops on peg 13M.

11 Lift the wristband off the pegs and weave about eight bands together (see the right inside cover) to make an extension so the wristband fits your wrist. Secure with a clip.

TIPS & TRICKS

When placing the rubber bands on the Rainbow Loom® be sure to follow the exact sequences given in the instructions and don't mix up the order of the bands on the pegs.

ESSENTIAL WEAVING TIPS!

Push the hook down through the groove in the peg and carefully pick up the bottom rubber bands to be woven through the ones above. Never touch or hold the rubber bands on the outside as this will stop them from weaving. Hold the hook with the crook facing away from you. You should be looking at the back of the hook, and the crook should be facing the inside of the peg. This way you won't get stuck on the top rubber bands when you try to pull out the hook.

You'll need an extension for some of the bracelet designs. This is explained on the back inside covers. In the instructions for the bracelet extension, we tell you that you will need eight rubber bands. If this makes the bracelet too loose or too tight for you, change the number of rubber bands to suit your wrist size.

Keep pushing the rubber bands down on the pegs between the various steps to make more room for the rubber bands that are yet to come. But take care not to change the sequence of the rubber bands.

If you find that some of the rubber bands come out of the bracelet when you lift it off the loom, this is probably because you didn't keep to the correct sequence when looping them or weaving them, or perhaps you missed a peg when you were weaving. To save rubber bands, you can just unpick the bracelet and start again from the beginning.

If you have any comments or queries regarding the instructions in this book, please contact us at enquiries@quadrille.co.uk.

Heike Roland & Stefanie Thomas
have been the „head sheep" of the BLACK SHEEP COMPANY since 2000. Their first book was published in German by frechverlag in 2004.
They spend almost the whole day sewing, knitting, crocheting, felting, sawing, drawing and designing practical and lovely things in their own inimitable cheery designs.
You can find out more about the latest news from the „black sheep" in their blog at http://black-sheep-company.blogspot.de. They're always delighted to welcome new additions to their flock!

THANK YOU!

Thanks are due to Herr Gerhardt of Supertoytrends for the Rainbow Loom® and to our models Benni, Charlie, Hanna, Helen and Moritz!

PUBLISHING DIRECTOR: JANE O'SHEA
COMMISSIONING EDITOR: LISA PENDREIGH
EDITORIAL ASSISTANT: HARRIET BUTT
CREATIVE DIRECTOR: HELEN LEWIS
DESIGN ASSISTANT: GEMMA HOGAN
PRODUCTION DIRECTOR: VINCENT SMITH
PRODUCTION CONTROLLER: STEPHEN LANG

Quadrille
craft

WWW.QUADRILLECRAFT.COM

FIRST PUBLISHED IN 2014 BY QUADRILLE PUBLISHING LIMITED
PENTAGON HOUSE, 52–54 SOUTHWARK STREET, LONDON SE1 1UN
WWW.QUADRILLE.CO.UK

FIRST PUBLISHED IN 2014 BY FRECHVERLAG GMBH

PHOTOGRAPHS © FRECHVERLAG GMBH, 70499 STUTTGART; LICHTPUNKT, MICHAEL RUDER, STUTTGART;
INSTRUCTION PHOTOGRAPHS © HEIKE ROLAND AND STEFANIE THOMAS
PRODUCT MANAGEMENT: ANJA DETZEL AND CAROLIN EICHENLAUB
PROOFREADING: MANUELA FEILZER, COLOGNE, AND ANNA BURGER
LAYOUT AND TYPESETTING: KATRIN KRENGEL AND ATELIER SCHWAB, HASELUND

ISBN: 978 184949 619 3

10 9 8 7 6 5 4 3 2 1

PRINTED IN SPAIN